When You Have a DREAM

30 DAYS OF DEVOTIONS TO EMPOWER THE DREAMER IN YOU

COMPILED BY

KISHMA A. GEORGE

When You Have A Dream;

30 Days of Devotions to Empower the Dream in You Copyright © December 2022
By K.A.G. (Kishma A. George Enterprises)
Published in the United States of America

by

ChosenButterflyPublishing LLC

www.cb-publishing.com
Cover design D'Vine Designs

ISBN: 978-1-945377-26-6

First Edition Printing

Printed in the United States of America

December 2022

Table of Contents

Day One

Impossibilities Don't Exist with God

by Tyneise Seaborough

Anything Is Possible

And being not weak in faith, he considered not his own body now dead, when he was about a hundred years old, nor yet the deadness of Sarah's womb.

Romans 4:19 (KJV)

Have you ever had a dream that was so big it made you nervous? Or it made you extremely happy but you had no idea how it would ever come to pass because it seemed humanly impossible?

If so, you're in great company.

Abram, at the age of 99 years old, had an encounter with God. Genesis 17:4–6 (NIV) reads, 4"As for me, this is my covenant

1

with you: You will be the father of many nations. 5No longer will you be called Abram; your name will be Abraham, for I have made you a father of many nations. 6 I will make you very fruitful; I will make nations of you, and kings will come from you.

But here's the problem, he's 99 years old and his wife is barren! The idea of Sarai having a baby at the age of 90 was so impossible that he laughed. But he never factored in the power of the Word of God. Let's face it, her eggs were no good and she was way too old. The entire situation was hopeless. It would require a miracle. But can I remind you that this is God's specialty? He specializes in making impossibilities possible. The term impossibility doesn't even exist with Him. What situation in your life is prophesying that everything is too old, dead, hopeless, it's not working, and that it's too late? Even dead things God calls back to life! He has the keys to hell and death. He conquered death and rose in three days. He has the victory over death. It's time for you to arise out of the pit, out of despair, out of hopelessness, and into victory! You are more than a conqueror through Christ Jesus.

God is giving you an opportunity today to partner with Him and act just like Him. He wants you to open your mouth and continually declare the Word of God to that situation. When there was darkness, God called forth light. When there was a storm, Jesus declared peace. When the fig tree didn't produce, He cursed it at its root. When Lazarus had died, He called Lazarus forth.

Are you ready to behold your dream? Are you ready to operate like your heavenly Father and get results like Him? If so, it's time to speak the Word only until you see it come to pass.

There are shackles being broken right now and chains falling off of you! I thrust you forward into the realm of possibilities.

PRAYER

Father, help me not to be moved by my situation and to walk by faith and not by sight until I behold the promise. I choose to partner with heaven today and call those things that be not as though they were in Jesus' name. Amen.

Day Two
Spiritual Projection

by Fedora Elie Ndovie

"I see men like trees" the blind man replied. The questioned posed was, "Can you see anything?" and the man looked up and had this reply. Then Jesus laid his hands on him again. And his sight was restored clearly in Mark 22–26. This blind man spent most his life with no sight. He walked around but could not see where he was headed. Most of us have learned to function blindly or with blurry vision. No target or little precision. So the question is can you see anything? What has been bubbling in your spirit? When God begins to open a vision or a dream it can leave you restless. He will send people, perfect strangers with a message. Sometimes He will communicate His will even in dreams. As He did with Joseph the dreamer in Genesis 37. I remember when I was contemplating going back to school for nursing. Since age 14 I would always go to nursing homes and be a companion for the

5

elderly. I would sing, read and chat with them. Especially about the Word of God. I didn't think anything much of it.

Some would say, "You will be a good nurse."

Others would say, "You are such a nice pastor."

And I thought, No way, I'm not that smart or that holy for that matter. But as a child I did wish secretly to be a nurse. I tried to patch up my siblings and friends when they were hurt. Later, I went into other endeavors. However, at some point in my adulthood the Lord brought me back full circle. The need to return back to school for nursing tussled with me and I kept coming across people who had information for schools and jobs that were hiring. I didn't realize God was speaking. The hardest step was getting started. It was not easy, but with prayer, family and friends' support I got through it as a divorced single mom. My sister Claudine stood close by me with the help of my son Theo along with Theo's two grandmothers, Sullyte and Sonnie. There were times when I did not know how I would pay the bills. Perfect strangers would just say they felt the need to give me a gift. It would be the exact amount I needed. My best friend, Corrine, would check in all the time to find out if I was okay financially. In Genesis 22:14 Abraham calls the Lord Jehovah Jireh (Yahweh provides). We have got to have faith in the vision and trust God the provider in the process. When I was following this dream to be a nurse all I did was calculate what I had in my hands. Father God showed me what was in His hands. Today I stand as a nurse. I also should mention that shortly after nursing school I was ordained as a pastor. Now I travel across the globe to preach the gospel. I also preach on radio and TV. To God be the glory. I could not see the vision in the beginning. It was reaching too far for me. Although the Lord was sending different ones to speak into my life I could not see it. We all have purpose. Some at a greater capacity than others. The Lord will lay the vision on our hearts in the form of a passion or burden. When He does we need to have 20/20 vision. Though things may get murky, foggy and stormy, causing the vision to look farther than close, we will not lose focus. When it begins to look blurry, go back to Jesus and ask Him to lay hands on your eyes again until your vision is restored clearly. Trust me, my friend; you will do more than you could ever imagine.

PRAYER

Dear Heavenly Father, give me 20/20 vision for your will for my life. Forgive me when I did not trust you enough. Lord, help my unbelief in the things you showed me and the messengers you sent to talk to me. Help me to be still and know you are God during adversity. May I not grow weary and faint but continue to push through in Jesus' Mighty Name.

Day Three

Interpreter of Dreams

by Tiffany McCullough

The purpose of this chapter is to encourage you to become the interpreter of your dreams. An interpreter is someone who is able to communicate and translate the heart of God concerning His divine will and purposes for one's life, future, or destiny. So many times we find those that are lost, disconnected, led astray, and/or deceived because they fail to commune with the Father. Communion establishes an intimacy of fellowship where the Father communicates His heartfelt desires for His people. This is not to deter you or anyone else from seeking Godly counsel; however, it is imperative that you entrust God on new levels, even if it appears as if He is not in control. You must rest assured, knowing that God is all-knowing and all-seeing. He has your back!

I believe there are moments in our lives when we face positions that challenge us to compromise our faith in God. The lives of Daniel, Shadrach, Meshach, and Abednego are examples of dedication and commitment. They were determined to serve God, regardless of the consequences. They did not give into the pressure around them. As you take a look at the Word of God in Daniel 3:16–17, Shadrach, Meshach, and Abednego said something very profound, which translated the heart of God towards wicked men. Standing erect, firm, and unwavering to serve another God, they confidently declared their commitment by interpreting their future. They uttered these words:

"O Nebuchadnezzar, we do not need to defend ourselves before you in this matter. If we are thrown into the blazing furnace, the God we serve is able to save us from it, and he will rescue us from your hand, O King. But even if he does not, we want you to know, O King, that we will not serve your gods or worship the image of gold you have set up. I believe very often in life there are moments we have to interpret to the enemy, the word of the Lord over our lives. So often many born again believers douse down who they are, because they have not been the interpreter of their own dreams and destiny. The Father says, For I know the plans I have for you, declares the Lord, plans to prosper you and not to harm you, plans to give you hope and a future."

Jeremiah 29: 11

You, my dear beloved, have a great purpose and destiny. It's understood that life brings moments of uncertainty, as it did for Daniel and his friends. But one thing you need to know and understand is that you are the interpreter of your future. Whatever

God has established shall be so; therefore, we must learn how to walk this walk and translate the victories already won by the Blood of Jesus. The Father gave you a dream, vision, and promise. Interpret it well and follow the blueprint set before you. God's Word and your faith are all you need as an interpreter of dreams.

PRAYER

Heavenly Father, I thank You for Your Word concerning me. I understand that my life is not my own; it belongs to You. Father, I yield my will in order to obtain every promise You have spoken over me. I declare that I shall live and not die to declare the Word of the Lord. Father, I believe every word spoken shall come to pass, as I open my mouth to interpret and decree my destiny!

Father, You are faithful and Your love has encompassed me. You shall direct my path and Your Word shall cover me. Amen

Day Four

Words Are Life

by Novita C. George

Finally, brethren, whatsoever things are true, whatsoever things are honest, whatsoever things are just, whatsoever things are pure, whatsoever things are lovely, whatsoever things are of good report; if there be any virtue, and if there be any praise, think on these things. Philippians 4:8 KJV

You have heard the adage, "Sticks and stones may break my bones, but words will never hurt me." It is thought that words will never hurt someone because they can't inflict bodily harm. They can't cut you and make you bleed. They can't give physical pain. However, speaking in general, words can and will give you physical, mental, psychological, spiritual and/or even emotional pain. If someone does not want to inflict any hurt on anyone then he/she should speak God's Word. Speaking the Word of God will always do nothing but good in all situations.

John 1:1 states (KJV), "In the beginning was the Word, and the Word was with God, and the Word was God." "In Him was life (v4)." Therefore, speaking the Word is speaking "life" because the Word is God and God is life. We should always speak the Word of God because it will infuse into someone's life growth, lifeblood, excitement, peace, energy, soul, heart, just to name a few. In other words, "Whatsoever things are true, whatsoever things are honest, whatsoever things are just, whatsoever things are pure, whatsoever things are lovely, whatsoever things are of good report (Philippians 4:8 KJV)," you speak those things.

QUESTION TO PONDER

Do I speak life in spiritually dead people?

PRAYER

God, help me to be discerning to know whom to speak Your Word to when opportunity comes my way.

Day Five
Purpose by Design

by Fedora Elie Ndovie

On earth as it is in heaven. Then what does heaven look like? Absolutely nothing like the human mind could fathom or think. When God created you and I, it was nothing like what the human could ever fathom or think. Which is what makes us unique. No matter how much "they" say we look like our kin. What God placed inside you, the hidden treasure in a plain vessel, will not look like me or anyone else. In order for us to move into the place of "purpose by design" to fulfill our destiny there are few things we must understand. First, you are His masterpiece. Yes YOU! Even with the crooked teeth, squeaky voice, knock knees and sweaty palms. According to Ephesians 2:10; "For we are God's masterpiece. He has created us anew in Christ Jesus, so we can do the good things He planned for us long ago." Which means the very best was put in you. The Lord did nothing less

15

than excellence in you. Now, you may not feel excellent, but it does not take away the fact that you are made in excellence. Secondly your purpose did not begin when you stumbled upon your AHA! moment. God the Creator knew you before you were formed in your mother's womb (Psalms 139). So the gifts, talents and skills were placed in you for appointed times to be revealed. We have a God that knows how to take darkness and void and turn it into beauty and purpose. Creativity and innovation are knit into the very fiber of your DNA. For we are made in God's likeness and image. The wittiest invention can be birthed in time of total adversity. You're not the keeper of time knowing when your purpose, vision and destiny will be unveiled. This is what separates us from God Supreme.

Lastly, God has been grooming you for your purpose since you were born. Unfortunately, many times we incur opposition from destiny killers. Our destiny killers can come from poverty, lack, abandonment, rejection, lack of education, fatherless and/or motherless homes etc. We tend to think that only the silver spoon or trust fund babies prosper. Yet why do the educated rich and wealthy people find themselves in drug rehabilitation? The spirit of void doesn't discriminate housing. It can find a place to live in whomever it wants. Whatever you didn't have or whom didn't have you is yesterday. The Lord didn't allow them to stay for a reason. The door of opportunity was shut for a reason bigger than you understood. Yes it hurts! You may even contemplate suicide. I was there too. But what I learned... We have to circumvent through life's labyrinth. When things can no longer get fixed with our natural hands, we use our spiritual hands to pray and ask God for direction. We search the Word of God for understanding. He

16

may answer in five minutes. Or you may "see" your answer in five years. He does answer. There will be some obstacle courses. Because of those obstacles know you'll be stronger and wiser when you get where you're going. SO NO MORE EXCUSES, my friend. It's time to walk into your purpose-filled destiny!

PRAYER

Our Father who art in Heaven. Hallowed be thy name. Thy Kingdom come. Thy will be done in my life on earth as you have written it in Heaven. Forgive me and help me to forgive others including myself for not being in the place I need to be. Lord, make your vision for me clear. I open myself up to what you have in mind for me. I submit to your process in Jesus' Mighty Name.

Day Six

God's Plans Not Yours

by Claudine Noel

"Be patient", "trust God", "have faith"; "are you sure God told you or called you to this?" "do you even have the funds for this project?" "I think you should drop this because it's (insert time spent on vision) and nothing has happened." Those may be the words/statements that you have been hearing since starting your journey of entrepreneurship, birthing the vision God laid on you or even pursuing another degree. Whatever it is that you know that God has called you to, to manifest in the earth realm, know you are not the first and will not be the last.

God has given you (yes You!) the vision and idea because God knows what He has placed inside of you. In Jeremiah 29:11 it reads, "For I know the plans I have for you," declares the LORD, "plans to prosper you and not to harm you, plans to give you hope and a future." This was God speaking to the people of Israel who

19

were in exile. While the children of Israel were in a foreign land, God is comforting them, letting the Israelites know, though you are not in the comfort of your land, you have left precious things behind, and you are not accustomed to the laws of this new land don't worry. Don't worry because I have a plan for you all, I have this all mapped out for your survival and success. In verse 12 God continues by giving the people instruction: "Then you will call on me and come and pray to me, and I will listen to you." If the people of Israel humble themselves and come to God and pray to Him, communicate with Him, He will listen, He will hear their cries and complaints.

In Ps. 18:6 David says, "In my distress I called to the LORD; I cried to my God for help. From His temple He heard my voice; my cry came before Him, into His ears." Remember God gave you the vision, the idea because He has a bigger plan for you and that little idea that has been taking space in your mind, heart and soul. Since He chose you to lead this portion of the plan, trust that He has everything you need. Just position yourself in Him, call upon Him as Hannah did, when she was seeking her own child; through her seeking, the prophet Samuel was born. We can add Madam C.J. Walker who became the first black self-made millionaire, Martin Luther King, Jr., the leader of the Civil Rights movement. To my cousin-sister, Mrs. Fedora Ndovie who through a failed divorce and countless dark storms trusted God, sought God, held on to her faith; she is now a Licensed Practical Nurse, remarried and a giant in the Kingdom of God. And my newfound inspiration, Dr. Kishma A. George, a pillar in the Kingdom of God, whose trust and faith in God birthed her to be a midwife to those coming up in this new generation. Every person named sought God and trusted God, despite of what others around them were saying to them or behind them.

Through the act of seeking God you shall come to know the plans that He has for you; through seeking God who is all power, you shall gain strategic and prophetic insight into the new move to pull you into your next. Go forth today seek God, put the idea, the vision, that you know that He gave you back in His hands and wait on Him, don't move without Him because all that you are looking for is in His plans for you

PRAYER

Father, in the name of Jesus I thank you for knowing the plans and having a plan for me. Tailored just for me, synchronized with the Kingdom plans just for me. I ask that you would give me strength today. Strength to seek in every part of this vision that you have given me. Help me to be patient in you, help me not to move in my own power, nor my own might. But I shall trust you. And I shall remember that you gave me this plan not just for me but for those who are coming up behind me. Father, I thank you for pulling my faith into a new level. I thank you for this vision, but most of all, I thank you for your love that you have for me. In Jesus' name I pray, Amen.

Day Seven

Faith It When You Have a Dream

by Dr. Deborah Allen

But without faith it is impossible to please him: for he that cometh to God must believe that he is, and that he is a rewarder of them that diligently seek him.

Hebrews 11:6

I hear the mighty roar of faith and expectation that is falling upon and all around us. It's the time to have massive faith that is relentless and gives us the ability to stand and know that nothing is impossible to us. Hold strong in your faith for it shall bring to pass the dreams you refuse to give up on. For without faith it's impossible to please God. You have to believe God for whatever you're asking Him for or it will never happen. Your faith is a powerful force that will lead, guide, direct and perfect your life. Without question, you must have faith when you have a dream.

23

The bigger your dream the bigger you should press in with your faith. Faith is the very thing that will move the hand of God. Hold on to your faith and keep on hoping. Do not give up when you have a dream. *I believe, I believe, I believe, I believe* is vibrating through my very being like a mantra for my life. You have to faith your dreams into existence for if you believe long and hard those dreams will come to pass. Faith your dreams, goals and vision; do not give up on what you believe will happen. Guts will be needed as you are wielding your faith. Faith will give you the strength to push, persevere, overcome and win at everything you put your hands to. Stand in faith; be strong and fierce when you have a dream!

PRAYER

I decree by faith miracles are happening in your life. May God's love flow fresh and exceed every expectation that you have. I declare you will see the rewards of your faith presently throughout your existence. I prophesy that your faith has entered you into a new dimension in God, which has allowed you to grow spiritually. Your latter is greater and God's goodness is increasing in every area of your life. I decree from the north, south, east and west that money cometh and meet every need for your dreams in this season. Today, your life will never be the same for your faith has brought you a beautiful life.

Day Eight
Faith is Your Power Gift

by Claudine Noel

Did you know that Faith is a power gift? Faith is the belief or trust in something or someone1. It is through your faith, the belief in and trusting God, that your goals, plans and achievements can come to fruition. There are nine types of Spiritual Gifts that we in the body of Christ can identify vividly in I Cor 12:6–10. They are the Word of Wisdom, the Word of Knowledge, the Gifts of Healing, the Gift of Faith, the Working of Miracles, the Gift of Prophecy, the Discerning of Spirits, Different types of Tongues and Interpretation of Tongues. These Gifts are broken down into three categories.

Revelatory Gifts: God The creator of the universe revealing His truth to man.

Word of Wisdom

Word of Knowledge

The Gift of Prophecy

Inspirational Gifts: Brings God's anointing and His blessings to the church.

The Discerning of Spirit

Different Types of Spirits

Interpretation of Tongues

Power Gifts: God imparting His divine powers and abilities to man. These gifts involve supernatural abilities and energy that man does not naturally possess.

Gift of Faith

The Gifts of Healing

The Working of Miracles

I went into great detail to help you understand how important your faith is and how much power you hold through your faith, to achieve many great things in this earth realm. You hold a great gift that can tear down walls. Physical walls, mental walls, emotional walls, and spiritual walls that keep you from taking the next step into whatever it is that you are creating, into whatever business that you're developing; taking the next step into the nonprofit that you know will help the community, state that you live in, most of all the world. The great thing that I love about this power gift is you don't need much. In Matthew. 17:20 Christ declares, "If you have Faith as small as a mustard seed you can say to this mountain move from here and it will move, nothing will be impossible for you." With a little bit of faith. A tiny bit of faith, smaller than a drop of rain. You can tell the mountains that are in front of you, that are behind you, that are on your left and the right side to move. Move! Move! Move! Knowing and trusting that the God of the universe, who gifted you with this power, gift of faith has anointed you to move in the earth realm as a giant. As a giant to move the mountains, to break the walls around your vision, to defeat the enemy wherever it is that he is trying to cause you to stumble to stay stagnant to feel defeated. I implore you to look up the mustard seed. See for yourself how much you Faith is required of you, to move into your next phase of GREATNESS! May the Lord open up your spirit and allow you to see how powerful you truly are just by having a tiny bit of Faith.

PRAYER

Father. Today, I ask that you help me walk in the spirit and the gift of Faith. Lord, help me to have Faith as small as a mustard seed so that I may be able to take giant leaps in the earth realm. Lord, may my Faith in you and your promises grow evermore not just today but forever. In the name of Jesus, I pray. Amen.

Day Nine
F.A.I.T.H

by Claudine Noel

AS you go throughout your day, meditate on the word Faith see where in your daily tasks you can begin to apply this power gift. Faith=Full Assurance In The Heart & Full Access Into The Heavens

Recently we talked about having faith as small as a mustard seed. With that measurement of faith (or a bigger measurement for some) you have come to understand that you are a powerhouse in the spiritual realm. As you grow and mature in your faith, believing God for the plans and the gifts He has for your life, we must begin to exercise Patience while working towards the vision. Just like a farmer believes (having faith) when a seed is planted there is a waiting period (having patience). During this waiting period the seed is nestling deep into the soil as the farmer is tending(working) to the ground above by watering the ground, making sure there is no foreign matter to disturb the ground; the seed is able to break out of its shell and begin to spread its roots to be strong enough to break through the soil to be activated by the rays of the sun and drops of water to become the flower, fruit, vegetable that was packaged in the form of a seed. The farmer cannot see what was planted without having patience, tending to the ground, and letting the seed go through its process.

James 2:20 says, "But do you want to know, O foolish man, that faith without works is dead?" The Apostle James is telling us, faith is not just trusting and believing, we must put some work in as we are implementing our faith and practicing patience. Just like the seed and the farmer, we must exercise our patience through our faith in God while still doing our part in building the vision that God has given to us. Today, as you begin to tackle the list of ideas and tasks concerning the vision, plan, mission that God has placed on your life, remember as you stand faithful on what the Lord has shown you, begin working first in prayer asking God to show you the steps you need to take for the next phase of the vision He has given you. After be still—patient—in God knowing that He is fighting for you (Exodus 14:14) so that the vision He has given you will manifest in the earth realm.

PRAYER

Heavenly Father, forgive me for not having patience in you; forgive me, O Lord, for thinking that it is by my own might and my own power that the vision you have given me would come to pass. Help me to seek you for prophetic strategies pertaining to the vision you gave me; in Jesus' name I pray Amen.

Day Ten

The Dreamer Who Works and Believes

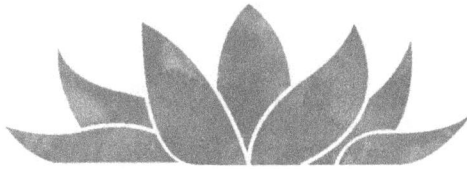

by Shamika Minisee

The dreamer in you stands on workable faith, meaning the dreamer believes and works towards seeing that dream to fruition. The dreamer knows not to worry because the Bible tells us in James 2:17, "Even so faith, if it has no works, is dead, being by itself." The writer's words equip us with the ability to be free and the strength towards that freedom. I want you to know that, as much as you have faith, you should find freedom in the work that you do knowing that God will provide all that you need and that Jesus was set apart to pave the way for you.

James tells us that faith is more than knowing, it's doing. It's present and active not yielding. So dreamer, let's activate that workable faith because we know who holds our hands!

PRAYER

Precious Lord, I thank you that the dreamer in me is awakened. Father, let me remember that faith and work co-exist and may I have the strength, Precious Lord, to walk the path you have set for me. Father, equip me to remember who I am and whose I am and that my every need is already laid out in front of me. Dear Father, show me your Faith by your Works. Amen

Read Verses:

James 2:18

James 2:22

Day Eleven

Move the Water

by Novita C. George

Ask, and it shall be given you; seek, and ye shall find; knock, and it shall be opened unto you:

Matthew 7:7 KJV

The little three-to-four-year-old girl, enveloped in her beach ring, wanted desperately to go to her mother who was a distance from her in the water. She called out to her mom to come and get her. Her mom remained where she was but called out, "Come to me! Move the water!" Without any hesitation, and with trust, the little girl moved the water with her little hands and arms while she steadily kept her eyes on her mom. She made swimming motions without realizing what she was doing. When she reached her mom, she had a radiant glow of satisfaction on her face. She had succeeded in her great desire to be with her mom!

Just like this little girl, you can accomplish whatever you desire in life. This little girl let her mom know what she wanted. You too must let God know your heart's desire. He will give you instructions to follow. However, to follow the instructions, you will have to trust Him. To develop a trust in Him you will need to receive Him as Your Lord and Savior, thus helping you to form a needed relationship with Him. You will become familiar with Him. He will not be a stranger to you. Then you will be ready with trust to listen to Him, when He gives instructions, keeping your eyes on Him, as you obediently follow. The results will be nothing less than success! You do want to be successful don't you?

QUESTIONS TO PONDER

Do you have a dream? Do you need help? Ask God today to help you with it.

PRAYER

Dear Heavenly loving Father, I want to_____
Please help me focus on You, to listen and follow Your instructions to become successful. Thank You, Jesus!

Day Twelve

There Must Be Vision When You Have A Dream

Dr. Deborah Allen

"And the LORD answered me, and said, Write the vision, and make it plain upon tables, that he may run that readeth it."

Habakkuk 2:2

Ohhhh weee, hear the warrior call that is reaching out to every dreamer on a global frequency. We have entered into the time when we may and can run with our visions! This is the now moment for your vision to take wings and soar past every limit that has ever been put upon your life or dreams. Now is the time for you to take the time to envision, embrace, write and run after your dreams with fierce tenacity to achieve them. Having true ability to see will provide clarity in your life to where you are going and what you can accomplish. Undisputedly, everything you are

35

seeking is already seeking you! When you have a dream, recognize that vision is an extremely crucial element in having a plan to live out your dreams. Vision along with clarity will allow you to achieve the impossible. Fresh vision is now bubbling throughout you so you can now begin to dream again. That means you must be able to see before you see when you have a dream. Without vision you will never know who, what or where you are going or what you will accomplish. Your eyes are now clear so you run like never before. When you have a dream, imagine it, dream it, write it, visualize it and finally fiercely run after it.

PRAYER

I decree God's supernatural blessings over your life. His divine words are currently birthing forth greatness into every area of your life. May the floodgates of dreams, witty ideas, inventions even businesses rain down fresh in your life. Even now there is an explosion of renewed vision with expanded dreams being released. May God's grace and favor be imparted into you in this season of your suddenly. Be elevated, your coast be enlarged on every side. I declare when you have a dream, it shall manifest in your life.

Day Thirteen

Faint Not, Dreamer, God Is Right Here

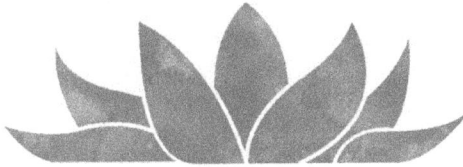

by Shamika Minisee

The psalmist says, "The Lord is my shepherd, I lack nothing."

Dreamer, this passage is all you need! I understand that you were born into a world that has thrown so much on you and scrambled your mind so much that your first thought is to worry. Faint not! If God is your shepherd, then everything you need is within. It is written! It is so! Dreamer, today, vow to take your joy back, to break through the pain and to have peace because God is your shepherd and if you follow God, He will restore your soul. Dreamer, on your darkest and brightest days, you lack nothing. Dreamer, on days when you feel so consumed that you just can't see the end, remember, He guides you along the right path. Dreamer, when you can't figure it out, remember your cup overflows. Dreamer, even when you must walk along, remember, you have comfort.

PRAYER

My God, thank you, for I realize that I am a manifestation of Psalm 23. God, I am thankful that you are my Shepherd and I was chosen as one of your sheep. May I never faint another day in my life because where the spirit of the Lord is, there is freedom. God, I pray that every soul on Earth realizes that they too are a manifestation of Psalm 23 and, like David, may we find goodness in dwelling in your Kingdom. Amen.

Verse: Psalm 23: 1–6

Day Fourteen
Work Your Plan

by Claudine Noel

Take a deep breath. Do that for about a minute. Say a quick prayer asking God to quiet your soul. (You can pray-Mind be still and know that He is God, body be still and know that He is God. You can repeat that a few times until you feel settled). Now let us begin!

Earlier we touched on faith, we learned how faith is a power gift. Faith is a weapon given to us by God to combat the lies that the enemy throws at us. Faith is the foundation of many success stories. From biblical times to the generation of our time. Billionaires and millionaires had faith in an idea and/or a product. They trusted in the mechanics or theories of the idea. The faith level that was produced due to a thought of something that did not exist was not invented, created, or thought of either. However, it was gifted to us. In Hebrews 11:1 it says, "Faith means being sure of the things we hope for and knowing that something is real even if we do not see it", NCV. Paul, the writer of Hebrews, wrote to the Jewish people sharing with them the concept of faith. To have faith, it is an act of trusting. Trusting in things you cannot see, feel, or touch. I always like to use the example of oxygen. We need oxygen to breathe in order for us to live. We cannot see the molecules that make up the oxygen, we can't feel it nor touch it, but we know it is there. We trust in this invisible element that keeps us alive with no doubts and fears, we never stop to think twice about it. We just get up and go. Well, that is how we should immerse ourselves in this great sea called faith. We need to just get up and go knock on the door, make that phone call, just start writing with no topic. Just get up and go! Be sure in the things you cannot see yet but are hoping to come into fruition. Remember, faith without works is dead.

We have a part in making sure the vision comes alive. Be the oxygen molecule for your vision, help it to breathe by praying over it daily, by giving thanks to God in advance for the lives of people that it will touch. Sow on the vision now; whether its seed of time or money. Begin to operate as though the vision has been birthed already in the earth realm. Don't sit on what God has given to you too much longer. Someone else may catch the vision and soar with it. Don't let time pass you by. You have power, you have many weapons, strategies given to you by God to achieve the dream in your lifetime. Leap into God's arms, put on the armor of God and shield yourself with faith. Patiently wait for His instructions as you seek Him for strength, comfort, and guidance. May the peace God along with His love and mercy be ever multiplied over you in this season of your journey to the Kingdom in Heaven. Amen

PRAYER

Dear heavenly Father. I thank you for being with me in these last five days. Teaching me and instructing me how to be faithful and patient, on how to seek you and to leap into what you have given me to be manifested here in this earth realm. Lord, I give you back this vision, this plan, this idea, this dream. May your will be done over it. May the lives of your people be changed forever more. May those who have never heard of you, Father, come to know who you are as their light and their salvation. May you continually reign across and over this Earth realm. Father, I love you. In Jesus' name I pray, Amen.

Day Fifteen

Weeds, Weeds, and More Weeds

by Novita C. George

All scripture is given by inspiration of God, and is profitable for doctrine, for reproof, for correction, for instruction in righteousness:

Timothy 3:16 KJV

I am surrounded with crotons and flowered plants in the front of my home. In the back, I have fruits and vegetables such as pigeon peas, guavas, sugarcanes, pomegranates, soursops, sugar apples, papayas, bananas, and okras. I am the one and only one to tend to all of my plants. In the past I have experienced loss of plants because of the use of the weed eater used by hired men to clean my yard. Now I clean the entire yard and hire someone to clean outside of my fencing. I do not mind getting my hands dirty. In fact, I love the feeling of dirt in my hands. I usually sit down on my big bathing pan. I even speak to them releasing my carbon dioxide as I inhale oxygen from them. I must weed often to remove grassroots and regular unwanted plants that have tendency to wrap themselves around the roots on my plants. Removing them saves my plants from getting suffocated and not growing. Worst scenario, the plants will eventually die. Removing the weeds allow the plant to grow to its full height.

One day, as I was weeding around one of my banana plants, I pondered and compared the life of the banana to Christians. Like the weeds, if we allow things that are not good for our minds, those same unhealthy, ungodly things will suffocate our spirit and stop us from growing spiritually. Worse, we can end up dead spiritually. It is important to weed out all ungodly things regularly from our lives so that we can grow and mature to our full potentials. Let's surround ourselves with godly things (Ephesians 5:19, Colossians 3:16, Psalms 1:1 – 3, 2 Timothy 3:16 – 17, 2 Peter 3:18 Galatians 5:22 – 23, and James 1:22 – 25).

QUESTIONS TO PONDER

What weed(s) do you have in your life that is/are preventing you from growing spiritually? How can you remove the weed(s) out of your life?

PRAYER

I want to grow and mature in my Christian living. God, help me to recognize unhealthy, ungodly things in my life to weed them out.

Day Sixteen

Be Intentional

by Setsu McClendon

Let the favor of the Lord our GOD be upon us and establish the work of our hands upon us; establish the work of our hands!

Psalms 90:17

GOD will help you identify your purpose in life if you seek Him. Be mindful of the things you say, the things you do, and who you are around when you are aware of your purpose. To fulfill your purpose, you must involve yourself with things that are aligned with it. You should do things with purpose, for a purpose. Rather than focusing on anything that isn't aligned, block out everything that isn't aligned. You can receive all that God has for you if you maximize your gifts and talents to their full potential.

Be Intentional about What You Say

Don't underestimate the power of your words. Let the WORD of GOD be the guide of your life and do what he has given you to do. Your beliefs will be shaped, you will be uplifted, inspired, healed, and your emotions will be restored to a positive state. Building up your self-esteem and boosting your confidence through positive self-talk is a key step to achieving your purpose-driven goals. It is your words that can influence and transform your life and the lives of those around you. Speaking positive, powerful, loving, and inspiring words is the best course of action. Your positive speaking will soon bear fruit. There will be a flourishing and multiplication of your dreams.

Be Intentional about What You Do

Follow the instructions you receive from the Father without modifying them or deviating from them. You can use it as a blueprint for success. Taking classes and attending workshops will prepare you for your sphere of influence. Utilizing your talents and gifts will lead to many opportunities and doors opening for you in ways you never dreamed of.

Be Intentional about Who You Connect With

Identify a mentor who has achieved the goals you wish to achieve. You can use their words of wisdom to avoid mishaps and be your voice of reason. It is said that iron sharpens iron, so it is important to surround yourself with strong people. Surround yourself with people who share your values, not those who don't, since they will impede your progress. You are destined for greatness and will prosper in all that you do.

PRAYER

Father, I thank you in advance for establishing the work of my hands as I am obedient to your voice. Everything that my hands touch will prosper and bring Glory to your name. You will be at the forefront of my mind as I search for you in the WORD. It is my duty to speak your promises until they are evident in my life and to share the good news of who you are with others.

$\mathcal{D}ay$ $\mathcal{S}eventeen$

Am I Content?

by Dr. Kishma A. George

Be careful for nothing; but in everything, by prayer and supplication with thanksgiving, let your requests be made known unto God.

Philippians 4:6 KJV

Are you content with where you are with your dreams? If you are not, you need to be. You need to be content with whatsoever state your dream is in (Philippians 4:11). You need not fret but ask God for wisdom to assist you with the dreams that He has implanted in you DNA. Yes, He is the One who gave you the dreams that you are so passionate about. Be sensitive and alert to people He will send/use as the instrument to aid you in your dreams!

Every God-given vision will become real if we will only have patience. Visions are about God's will and not about us. Godly

49

visions can be frightening because they are so great. However, they become reality as we move in faithfulness. God gives great visions that only He can accomplish so that when they become reality God must receive all the glory! God is truly Faithful to His Word! I want every DREAMER today to believe that your DREAMS will come to pass! Remember, giving up is NOT an option! It's your time to DREAM BIG! It's your time to take LEAPS of Faith and pursue your God-given DREAMS! Don't get discouraged. Don't look at your age. Don't look at how long the dream is taking to manifest. Keep the faith and Believe God. In this NEW Season, you are coming out from being a Doubter to becoming a DREAMER! No more fear. No more delay! You will pursue your Dreams in this Season with boldness and confidence knowing that all things are POSSIBLE for God! It's your time to Bring FORTH THE DREAMER IN YOU! DREAM BIG!!!

PRAYER

God, I need help with my dreams! Give me the wisdom to recognize the help that You have sent/will send my way to be successful with my dreams. In the name of Jesus!

Day Eighteen
Here Comes That Dreamer

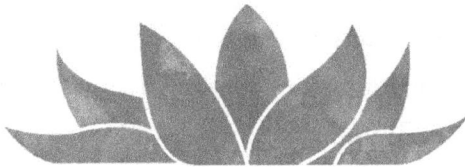

by Tiffany McCullough

Sometimes, the race to destiny is fraught with pitfalls and unwanted detours. We could never have anticipated the timeless seasons ahead. My memories are often triggered by Joseph, a young man who was given a dream from God in his youth. In contrast to what was expected, Joseph did not immediately experience the fulfillment of his dream. As a result, there were many trials and tribulations that he had to endure.

It is common for individuals to feel discomfort when they hear the words trial and tribulation because it implies an impending challenge. Many people are reluctant to willingly face difficult experiences that test their fortitude and strength. Nevertheless, this was exactly what Joseph faced.

Among my favorite stories in the Bible is the story of Joseph. Perhaps it is a favorite of yours as well. Joseph's story recounts many of the darkest moments in his life. He was betrayed by his brothers, enslaved, falsely accused, imprisoned for doing the right thing, and abandoned by his family. Besides these challenges, he encountered many others that challenged his faith.

Nevertheless, it led me to think about my own personal testimony and about the many people who will read this book—those who may feel defeated, think God has forgotten about them, or just want to give up. Allow me to encourage you, not with myths or fictitious tales or with false exultation over untrue demonstrations. Thus, I come to you with the Father's true heart and His desire to bless you. My writing is an expression of my personal testimony that the God of Abraham, Isaac, and Jacob will see you through!

We often hear sayings about the ways God will make, but if you look at the life of Joseph, his pain was necessary. Joseph's pain was one of the keys to his greatness. Although it may not always be clear what God's path for us is, as we may often take detours and lose sight of His divine plan, the Father will always find a way to reroute us and put us in alignment with His divine will.

The Word of the Lord says in Jeremiah 29:11, "For I know the plans I have for you says the Lord, plans to prosper you and not to harm you, plans to give you a hope and a future."

One of the things I love about Joseph is that he grew in his pain and developed despite suffering. He did not allow his current season to dictate the outcome of the daylight that would come.

When we observe nature's seasons, they are marked by distinctive weather patterns and periods of daylight, resulting from the earth's changing position in relation to the sun.

Thus, we correlate our lives in comparison to the seasons. Whether it's for the good or the bad, nothing remains the same. It is in the parched seasons that we learn to find water as our longing souls pant for the refreshing springs bursting forth within one's immaterial essence.

The dreamer conceives, giving birth through visions immersed in ideas of faith. "Here comes the dreamer!" they shout as God says, "You are the next Joseph!" Released with the robe of many colors, you are God's chosen and His elect! Get ready! Now shift!

PRAYER

Father, You are my hiding place in times of trouble. Though the enemy comes in like a flood, You, O God, shall lift up a standard before me. Thou, oh Lord, are a shield around me, my glory, and the One who lifts my head. Father, as You were with Joseph, so shall I succeed in everything I put my hands to do, so that my life may glorify You. Father, for every dream You've given me the doors shall be opened unto me! And as You caused Joseph to reign, so shall I rule in the land You have given unto me. I decree and declare that my children and everything from my loins are blessed. I hereby renounce every hidden agenda of my enemies; spirits of deception, falsehood, lies, schemes, evil plots, and harmful plans shall not overtake me! I decree that they are overthrown now by the power of Your Holy Spirit! Father, cause me to walk in the radiance of Your presence, exerting nothing but You. Father, I give You complete and total access. Take my will as I walk out my purpose and the divine path set before me. I declare that I am not only a dreamer but an atmosphere shifter and a demon-slaying servant sent to carry out Your will. So, I put on my robe of many colors as a sign of total submission to Your will. Amen.

$\mathcal{D}ay$ $\mathcal{N}ineteen$
$\mathcal{D}esiring$ $\mathcal{T}o$ $\mathcal{B}e$ $\mathcal{W}ise$

by Novita C. George

A wise man will hear, and will increase learning; and a man of understanding shall attain unto wise counsels:

Proverbs 1:5 KJV

I am a retired teacher who taught for 33 years in the public education system. I was in the habit of telling my students not to do something and always sealed it with my favorite adage. I loved to end my scolding with, "A word to the wise is sufficient." Believe me, I had no problem with them choosing what was proper and correct. The key word was "wise." They wanted to be labeled as being wise.

Proverbs 1:5 states, "A wise man will hear and will increase learning and a man of understanding shall attain unto wise counsels." Only fools despise wisdom and instruction (v7). If you want to be wise then you must be a good listener. You do not listen to any one but godly, righteous people. People who are wise. You will know who to listen to because God will give you the spirit to be discerning and know whether that individual is right with Him. You will need to have a relationship with God to begin with.

QUESTIONS TO PONDER

Am I being wise to listen to good advice to help me with my dreams? Am I receiving the best counsels for my dreams to come to fruition?

PRAYER

Father in heaven, please give me the desire to be willing to listen so that I can learn and become wise. May I be able to also discern good from bad counseling.

Day Twenty

Dream Killers

by Prophetess Shaunte D Haslem-Jones

Thou hast given him his heart's desire and hast not withholden the request of his lips.

Psalm 21:2

Have you desired something so badly that you visualize yourself with those desires? When you go to sleep at night you dream about your future. This is a word for the wise; don't expect people to believe in your dreams. Do not pay attention to the "Dream Killers"; the enemy will try to find a way to sabotage your dreams. Have you ever noticed that when you share your dreams with "Dream Killers" they talk negatively or are unresponsive? A "Dream Killer" doesn't want to see you shine because they don't have the courage or faith to go after their dreams. "Dream Killers" have the nerve to send you a video or post through a text or social media to brag on the "next man's" success. From this day forward, dream, pray, and have faith in God; there is nothing too hard for Him.

According to the Bible, in Gibeon the Lord appeared to Solomon in a dream by night and God said, "Ask what I shall give you" 1 Kings 3:5. Solomon asked for an understanding heart to judge the people and to discern good and evil. 1 Kings 3:9 God granted Solomon's request. God is waiting for you to ask; He is ready to show up and show out for you Hallelujah! The Lord showed up while Solomon was dreaming. God is a God of signs and wonders; the sign was the dream, the wonder was God asking the "dreamer Solomon's" request.

I would like to share my testimony to encourage you that dreams really come true. In all honesty, I was raised in a single parent low-income home, but I visualized myself having something out of life. I got pregnant while attending high school. The counselor recommended that I dropout of high school and get a GED because I did not pass the graduation tests. Hey, the odds were against me, but I had Faith in God and I refused to listen to the "naysayers". Nevertheless, I passed the high school graduation tests and received my diploma. I am the first one in my family to obtain a bachelor's degree while operating in multiple roles. Currently I am pursuing a master's in Divinity. As a result, I have co-authored three books. I am a wealth generator in which I have created a brand called "Divine Inspire" to mentor the youth using an Eight-Step Means-End approach. Lastly, please open your heart and receive this prayer.

PRAYER

Father, in the name of Jesus, anoint your child afresh right now. I bind the attacks of Satan's kingdom and loose liberty. Father, please restore the dreams and visions within your child. Father, increase the faith within your servant, you are our vindicator. Servant of God you will thrive in your talents and purpose. Father God, you are the God that gives good gifts to your children. The blessing of the Lord maketh rich and add no sorrow; therefore, Father God, shower your child with blessing.

Amen

Day Twenty-One

King David's Victory

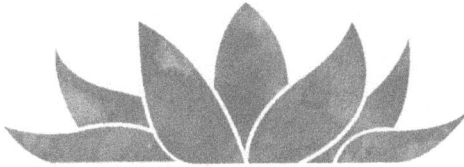

by Fedora Elie Ndovie

What's in your arsenal? King David was anointed and appointed to be king by God through the Prophet Samuel, another anointed and appointed vessel of God. With the horn of the oil was drawn the Spirit of the Lord came powerfully upon David in 1 Samuel 16. David was given the vision and was equipped to run with the vision. Yet he had to wait to get to the vision. It seemed very simple. However, spiritual "Opposition" and "Destiny Killers" were assigned to block and delay the process. They could not curse what God had blessed. Unfortunately, they can delay and create detours. What do you mean, didn't he become King? Yes, but there was a fight and struggle to get to the throne. God had been preparing David as a young warrior to be skillful in battle with the fiercest animals. This training would later serve him during a call to action. A fight with the fiercest man in the land, Goliath.

While others trembled, David prayed for anointing and wisdom. He had a strategy. From his arsenal he used some anointed smooth rocks that would tear down a great giant. David had the victory! And so his life would continue like this … battle, victory, warfare and victory. Alas the throne! He would ask the Lord should he pursue? The Lord would send David and he would see victory. Where is the Lord sending you? What are getting ready to pursue? Business, a new invention, ministry or an organization? Whatever the category may be, do you believe it is the Lord that has sent you? No matter how big or small every dream needs a strategy and achievable goals. You should understand there is a spiritual opposition that will show up to challenge your idea and your progress. In other words there will be a fight. It may even seem like it's people who are boxing you. Ephesians 6:12 states, "our struggle is not against flesh and blood, but against the rulers, against the authorities, against the powers of the dark world and against the spiritual forces of evil in the heavenly realms". Those spirits will influence people to work against you and your plans. 2 Corinthians 10:4 reminds us "the weapons of our warfare are not carnal, but mighty through God for pulling down of strongholds." Contend in the spirit for what is rightfully yours. For if God showed it to you it is YOURS! So what's in your arsenal? Are you prayed up? You will present your petition to God and declare victory over your plans. Have you emptied out by fasting? This helps you to be in tune with hearing from God (Ezra 8 21–23). Is your "sword" sharpened, which is the Word of God?" Knowing the Word of God is like going to court with your book of law in hand. You will know your rights. You will protect yourself against the accuser of the brethren, Satan. Understand

and declare Isaiah 54:17, "No weapon formed against thee shall prosper, and every tongue that shall rise against thee in judgement shall be condemn. This is the heritage of the servants of the Lord and the righteousness is of me, saith the Lord." What you carry in your arsenal is key to your victory for your dreams. Walk boldly to your victory, my friend! It belongs to you!

PRAYER

Dear heavenly Father, I thank you for your victory in Christ Jesus! I thank you that the battle has already been won for me. Bless me with the anointing that destroys the yolks of any bondage in my life. Transform me by renewing my mind from old negative ways of thinking. I declare VICTORY in my life, family, business, ministry, education and plans in Jesus' mighty name.

Day Twenty-Two

Never Disconnect from Who You Are

by Tiffany McCullough

Never disconnect from who you are. That one word alone says so much—disconnect. As I'm writing, I envision a cord plugged in an outlet that receives a transfer of electricity from the outlet into the appliance. A rapid draw on available power occurs. Considering this scenario of a plug and an outlet, it draws comparisons to us and the Father. When our lives are connected to Him, we receive the power surge to connect to others and set them ablaze.

This truth reminds me of a remarkable civil rights leader by the name of Dr. Martin Luther King Jr., who made a great impact on our nation. Dr. Martin Luther King was known for his civil rights movement against segregation. He delivered some of the most iconic speeches. He fought for justice through peaceful protest. But one of the things I love about Dr. Martin Luther

King Jr. is this—he never disconnected from who he was. He knew his purpose and came to fulfill it.

One of the many profound statements he made was, "You can kill the dreamer, but you can't kill the dream." What a powerful sentiment! This statement expresses so much!

Therefore, always remember that you are so important to the Kingdom of God. Every threat against your life and destiny cannot stop the plan of God concerning you! The Word of God says, "For by you I can run against a troop, and by my God I can leap over a wall" (Psalm 18:29 ESV).

In this season of your life, you must get as radical as possible for God. Being radical is when you affect the fundamental nature of something; you begin to shake things up. And I believe in my heart that it is not by coincidence that you're reading this book. It was God's plan that this day and time would come when you would pick up this book, read profound stories, and hear testimonies of healing and deliverance. God had you on His mind before you even reached this point. There is nothing in your life that God is not concerned about; the purposes of the Lord shall be fulfilled through you. Every dream and promise shall come to pass. Never allow life to disconnect you from the Promise Keeper. Dream and dream big! The blueprint is already laid out for you.

PRAYER

Father, You are Lord of all. Our days are numbered by You. Father, each moment I live, breathe, and have my being, I consider all the ways You have made for me. I'm truly grateful that You would even consider me. You chose me when I didn't choose You. Yet, Your love for me caused me to draw near, only to discover a pure love that's so true. I'm amazed at how You cover me; Your Blood was shed on Calvary. Before I was born, You thought about how much You just wanted to care for me. Yet, the love I show can never compare to what I truly owe. Father, there's no greater love than Yours in all of this earth. Help me never to disconnect from my only true source, which is You. I love You. Amen.

Day Twenty-Three
Chick in the Yard

by Novita C. George

And call upon me in the day of trouble: I will deliver thee, and thou shalt glorify me.

Psalm 50:15 KJV

It was a quiet sunny day and I decided to work on the computer. It is not always quiet in the neighborhood due to loud music from an old Rasta man and young men adult Arabs. The quietness was broken with a chick's frantic cluck-cluck, cluck-cluck.... It clucked back and forth loudly in front of my yard. I heard no other, only one. I opened my living room door and stepped outside. There was the chick all by itself; it had gotten separated from its mother hen. I opened my gate, stepped back and it walked outside and there was silence. Quietness was restored!

Immediately, I thought about what we as people ought to do when we are trapped and want to be free. We ought to cry out for help from God and He will liberate us (Psalm 50:15). The Bible states, "My help comes from the Lord who made heaven and earth (Psalm 121:2). Ask and it will be given to you, seek and you will find (Matthew 7:7)." The chick cried and searched out for help, and I went out to free it to go and look for its mom. The chick represented us, and I represented God.

Do not allow pride to stop you from seeking God's help (Psalm 10:4) I like Biblereasons.com's quote, "Don't be shy about asking for help. It doesn't mean you're weak, it only means you're wise." Dwight L. Moody sums it up well, "Some people think that God does not like to be troubled with our constant coming and asking. The way to trouble God is not to come at all." It is okay to cry out for help for God is a very present help in trouble (Psalm 46:1).

QUESTIONS TO PONDER

How often should I seek God for help in time of trouble? Have you ever asked God to assist you in pursuing your dream(s)?

PRAYER

Heavenly Father, remind me to be mindful to look and seek Your help for challenges in my life.

Day Twenty-Four
Pray Your Way Through

by Setsu McClendon

Rejoice always, pray continually, give thanks in all circumstances; for this is God's will for you in Christ Jesus.

1 Thessalonians 5:16–18

It is the prayer that you will turn to during the different seasons that you will encounter on this journey that serves as your road map. During your journey, challenges will come to strengthen you along the way. During those challenging times, prayer will be essential to your survival. To locate your destination, you use MapQuest while driving. As for prayer, it guides you to GOD's ultimate destination for your life. You can expect great things from GOD if you stay on his path. Whenever you feel like giving up, pray. Don't be afraid to pray when you're unsure. Pray when things seem to be going against God's promises. You will gain more peace and guidance when you pray. It also gives you strength and endurance to keep going.

Whenever you feel like giving up, pray. A divine idea is always larger than you, so it's exciting to receive it. It's exciting to share the news with those who matter most to you. However, if you do not receive a positive response, your spirit is dampened. Several factors have contributed to a decline in enthusiasm and drive. You got the idea from God, so don't expect a fan club to celebrate your excitement. Don't let go of your excitement and energy until the project is completed. Never forget why you started; it serves as a reminder not to give up.

In times of doubt, pray. Doubt is natural for humans; instead of believing what GOD says, we believe what we see. Whether things go your way or not, you must believe they will. This is easier said than done, but it is the truth. When you doubt yourself, you are hindering your progress toward the purpose GOD has for you. No matter what obstacles you face, you will prevail and fulfill GOD's purpose for your life. Take what GOD has given you seriously and don't second guess it. It was clear that you heard God!

Pray when things are going against the promises of God. There will be times in your life when you will lose hope due to certain circumstances. There is a reward waiting for you on the other side, but you must believe that it is worth the effort. As you gain wisdom and knowledge, you will be able to encourage others. You will be able to comfort those linked to your purpose as GOD comforts you during challenging times. Try not to be distracted by the challenges and forget what God has promised you. Every day, every night, and forever, GOD remains the same.

PRAYER

If I have doubted what you have called me to do, please forgive me. Please grant me the wisdom, courage, and fortitude to accomplish what I have been given. I know you will do exceedingly and abundantly more than I could ever ask or think according to your power working within me. In Jesus' Name!

Day Twenty-Five

Accessing the Prophetic Promise

by Tyneise Seaborough

When God made his promise to Abraham, since there was no one greater for him to swear by, he swore by himself.

- Hebrews 6:13 (NIV)

Imagine drifting off to sleep at night, as is custom, but this time the Lord visits you by way of dream. He whispers in your ear the plans that He has for you. Vivid details of this movie playing before you reveal glimpses of His destiny for you. Mentally there has been an imprint engrained in the soulish part of you and your spirit man. And when you wake up, you share it with those who love you, your family. But to your surprise, they are envious and jealous. And they hate the dreamer in you.

Genesis 37:5 (NIV) reads, Joseph had a dream, and when he told it to his brothers, they hated him all the more.

Whew! His dream served as an agitator to those closest to him.

Dreams are like portals that have been opened up before you that are full of prophetic power, destiny, mysteries, and the security of your future. They are an expression of the Word of God for your life in the form of images. They are the imprint of God's Word or His voice in your vivid imagination.

Dreams are both powerful and impactful in that you are more likely to remember what you saw vs. what you heard.

Joseph had no idea that his dreams would thrust him into a place of hardship, warfare, and strife with his family. However, they spoke volumes, encouraged, and prophesied to him in the midst of every opposing situation and setback. His brothers plotted to kill him, but because of the prophetic promise that was declared over his life, the mercy of God stepped in via his brothers Reuben and Judah. The assignment of death was aborted and he was only sold into slavery, which, in turn, shifted him into perfect alignment with the plans of God.

Even when you don't understand what's going on in your darkest moments, the promise will serve as a catalyst for you. In Joseph's case, being sold into slavery, placed in prison, and being forgotten about all led to his promotion. In spite of each challenge, the Word revealed that the Lord was with Joseph.

So what's the challenge you're currently facing? What has God revealed to you? Are you willing to trust Him to the end?

I want to encourage you not to give up. Your prophetic promise is awaiting you; the door to your destiny is open! Keep moving forward and walk into it. Even David had to encourage himself when the people turned their backs on him and considered stoning him. Encourage yourself in the Lord and find you some spiritual cheerleaders.

PRAYER

May the Lord release your destiny helpers to assist you with the fulfillment of your promise. I decree and declare that you shall use wisdom and discretion and move forward with momentum in Jesus' mighty name. Amen.

Day Twenty-Six
Quit Worrying

by Novita C. George

And which of you with taking thought can add to his stature one cubit?

Luke 12:25-26 KJV

"My life has been filled with terrible misfortune (worries); most of which never happened," Michel de Montaigne claimed, five hundred years ago. Now there is a study that proves it. The study revealed that 85% of what the subjects worried about never happened. With the 15%, 79% found out that they could handle the difficulties better than was contemplated.

Worrying is not good for anyone's health. It can cause high blood pressure or even death. God does not want us to worry because it cannot add a single hour to our life's span(Luke 12:25). Matthew 6:25–26 states, 25 "Therefore I tell you, do not worry about your life, what you will eat or drink; or about your body, what you will wear. Is not life more than food, and the body more than clothes? 26 Look at the birds of the air; they do not sow or reap or store away in barns, and yet your heavenly Father feeds them. Are you not much more valuable than they?" Tomorrow will care for itself (Matthew 6:34). Be anxious for nothing, but in everything by prayer and supplication with thanksgiving let your requests be made known (Philippians 4:6). Stop worrying and cast all your anxieties on God because He cares for you (1Peter 5:7). If you have not given God all your worries, do so today! Do not DELAY!

QUESTIONS TO PONDER

What am I anxious for regarding my dreams? Have I given all my anxieties to God?

PRAYER

God, I am anxious about _____
Please help me to trust You and hand over all my worries about my dreams to You.

Day Twenty-Seven

Speak Affirmations

by Setsu McClendon

For we are GOD'S handiwork, created in Christ Jesus to do good works, which GOD prepared in advance for us to do.

Ephesians 2:10

It is God's plan for you to accomplish great feats! It is essential that you are confident in who you are to fulfill what God has called you to do. Regroup when you're feeling discouraged or burned out. Keep your motivation and focus high by saying, "I am," affirmations daily. It is your destiny to break down barriers!

AFFIMATIONS

I am loved and complete in GOD.

I am handpicked by the Father and redeemed.

I am thankful, grateful, patient and kind.

I am worthy of peace and happiness.

I am valuable, unique, and chosen.

I am forgiven, cherished, and blessed.

I am an ambassador for GOD and will speak with boldness.

I am a crown of beauty and part of a royal generation.

I am confident and powerful to do great exploits.

I am authentic and lives will be transformed by my story.

I am ready to accept divine connections.

I am healed, delivered, and set free from all negativities.

I am successful in every area of my life.

I am free from my past and will embrace my present.

I am open to receive all that GOD has in store for me.

I am seated in heavenly places with Christ.

I am a shining light and will utilize my gifts to advance the Kingdom.

I am worthy of new opportunities and will have an abundant life.

PRAYER

Father, I thank you that I am who you say I am. I will speak positive affirmations over my life to stay rooted and grounded in you so I can accomplish all you have for me to do.

Day Twenty-Eight

You Did It

by Claudine Noel

You did it! You took the leap into making up your mind and starting that project, business, non-profit, mending a broken relationship, whatever it is that you have decided to and started working on it—YOU DID IT! So many times, we say to ourselves, "By next time this year I am going to...." "I will be a...." only to find ourselves in the same place the following year. But the fact that you took one step to begin achieving your goals, one step to securing your purpose in the earth realm, that one step, was you telling all those that said, "you could not", or "you would never" that the God of the universe said you could, and you did. Phil 4:13

God, there is nothing you cannot achieve. Philippians 4:13 has become for some just words or a cliché said when one is going through a hard time. But in fact, when you pair your Faith in Jesus

Christ alongside this powerful statement and sentiment declared over the people in Philippi (Ph 1:1), there is an activation that begins to happen inside of you. Knowing that because you have been redeemed by the blood of the Lamb you are a Kingdom citizen. As a citizen you have rights, and with those rights to the Kingdom of God you have access to the Kingdom of God. Anything and everything that you need and or want is available to you through your faith in Him. It is by Faith in the promises of God that you will and shall attain your dreams and more.

PRAYER

Lord Jesus, may my faith grow in you more and more each day. My I remember as a Kingdom citizen I have access to your heavenly realm to attain the things I need to achieve my dreams and the matters of your Kingdom in the earth realm. In Jesus' name I pray, Amen!

Write down Three things you would like to accomplish today or by that end of the week.

1.

2.

3.

Remember if you undertook one of your three items you
are still one step away from your Goal.
Now go be great in the things of God! 😊

84

Day Twenty-Nine

It's Your Set Time

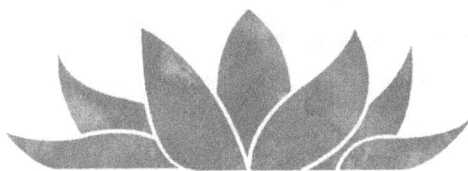

by Fedora Elie Ndovie

Kairos! Not just any time but NOW. The right time. As Jesus sat across from His mother, Mary, I can just imagine the silent tension that was growing between them. In John 2:1–12 The wedding at Cana called for the best of the best. I am pretty certain that much thought and planning went into the details of such a holy matrimonial celebration. And yet there arose a relatively crucial situation. They were out of wine. Mary knew she came with a special guest of honor that could fix the problem. She leans in to tug on Jesus like a mother would. "They have no wine," she whispered.

I believe that is also how God pulls on us to be an answer to a problem in the earth realm. Nonetheless, Jesus was not moved until He had heard from the Father to move. When God prompted Jesus, the anointing to do miracles came upon Him. Jesus was now prepared to perform His first miracle. Water turned into wine. Thirty years of preparation. His Kairos time arrived. The set time.

There is no mention that Jesus grew up in a vineyard and He was crushing grapes all His life. In fact, much of His life was spent in the temple learning and teaching the Word of God. Now the time of manifestation was present. Mary quickly told the servants "Do whatever He tells you to do." I could close this chapter right here. **Obedience not feelings.** It's not about how you feel but about what God told you to do. Many times, we get caught up in a feeling. As I am guilty.

There is an anointing that comes upon us for that Kairos time or season. This anointing strengthens you for the task. It covers and protects you from spiritual attacks of the enemy. 1 Peter 5:8 – 9 says, *Your adversary the devil prowls around like a roaring lion, seeking whom to devour. Resist him, standing firm in your faith.* The anointing comes with power and authority in Luke 10:19.

The difference between talent and anointing is anointing destroys the yokes, delivers and conquers. It's what David had as a warrior unlike others who formally trained in an army. They ran the other way when Goliath showed up. Anointing is what drove demons away from Saul when David played music. God has anointed you too for your set time. There is an office waiting for a CEO. There is a failing company that needs a manager to take them to the next level. There is a patient that is waiting for an innovative surgeon.

There is a person that is feeling like no one understands their unique situation they are waiting for a "how to move on" book from you! Yes YOU! God has anointed and appointed you for the position with little or no education. You may not even be formally trained. However, there is a supernatural anointing and grace that is upon you. Psalm 23 tells us that He anoints our head with oil, our cup overflows. What has God anointed you for in this season? What have people been telling you that you are really good at effortlessly? People may have pulled and tugged on you for a thing but today the Lord Himself is telling you through me "GO FORTH, DAUGHTER, GO FORTH, SON, IT'S YOUR SET TIME!" He has not given you a spirit of fear, but of power, love and sound mind. So run with your dream.

PRAYER

Heavenly Father, I thank you for fearfully and wonderfully creating me. I thank you for the excellence that is within me because you put your very best in me. Help me to see what you see, Lord. Obedience is better than sacrifice. Lord, help me to be obedient and harden not my heart when you or your messengers speak. Make my feet like hinds' feet and make me to walk upon my high places. I pray not to be late to my set time appointments in Jesus' mighty name.

Day Thirty

You Will Have an Overwhelming Joy

by Setsu McClendon

Our mouths were filled with laughter our tongues with songs of joy. Then it was said among the nations, The Lord had done great things for them. The Lord has done great things for us, and we were filled with joy.

Psalm 126:2–3

The dream GOD gave you does not require everyone to agree with it. The dream was designed for you to accomplish, and God trusts that you will do so. It is such an honor to have the Father download ideas and concepts for you to implement. Do not let fear, discouragement, or what you think you lack hinder you. To fulfill the dream, you have everything within you. For your instructions, you must be in harmony with the voice of GOD through His WORD and PRAYER. It will always be bigger than you! That means you must rely on the leading of our Father for the success of your dream. Don't forget that His blessing will accompany your work. The first step to moving forward will be to eliminate any hindrances.

A common method used by the enemy to keep you from progressing in the Kingdom is to paralyze you with fear. To prevent you from progressing in the Kingdom, the enemy often paralyzes you with fear. GOD has not given you a spirit of fear but of love, power, and a sound mind. As a result, you will be free of fear and have the courage to undertake the tasks GOD has given you.

When you are discouraged, it means you lose confidence, believing you won't be able to achieve your goals. Put small, attainable goals in front of you and surround yourself with positive people to regenerate your confidence.

Believe that you can do it! You will do it! You will be successful in GOD! You will prosper!

You will receive blessings associated with your dream from GOD. It is a known fact that God's WORD will not return void to Him. According to the Word, your mouth will be filled with laughter, making you feel as if you are dreaming. There will be great things done for you and through you by GOD. There will be an overwhelming feeling of joy overtaking you. Why? It was your willingness to please GOD that enabled you to obey the voice of GOD despite all the challenges you faced. It will amaze people to see GOD'S hand at work in your life, attracting them to Him. Other people will be inspired, encouraged, and motivated by your story. You have people waiting for you! Get up, brush yourself off, and get to work!

PRAYER

In advance, I thank you for fulfilling your promises in my life. Your blessings will enable me to bless others. I will spread the joy you give in my life to others, to advance the Kingdom. I know apart from you I can't do anything.

Meet the Authors

Dr. Kishma A. George

Dr. Kishma A. George can, in a single phrase, be described as a Purpose Pusher. She is an inspirational speaker, entrepreneur, prophetess, mentor, playwright, TV host, radio personality, producer and 8x best-selling author, and her overarching mission is to inspire people to fulfill their God-given purpose. Dr. Kishma's work as a speaker and mentor is executed through the Women Destined for Greatness Mentoring Program in Kent County, DE. She believes that despite life's circumstances, there is greatness inside of you! Dr. Kishma A. George is the President and CEO of K.I.S.H. Home, Inc., acronym for Kingdom Investments in Single Hearts (K.I.S.H.). K.I.S.H. Home Inc. was founded out of a desire to positively impact the lives of girls and women in the state of Delaware as well as those young women who are presently in or have aged out of the foster care system. While working as an Independent Living Mentor Dr. George witnessed the tremendous challenges that aged-out foster care youth experienced while trying to find their way to a self-sufficient and stable life. A passion within her grew for these young adults and their future as she experienced their frustration in handling basic skills, such as opening a checking/savings account, parenting and the frustration of single parenthood.

Dr. George knew that these young adults, whether they were a single parent or single, needed a strong support system that would empower and encourage them to take control of their lives. They struggled in their transition of leaving foster care because many were still attending high school and were not emotionally or financially stable. After witnessing this, Dr. George began her journey of seeking ways to assist young adults in becoming emotionally and economically self-sufficient so that their transition out of the foster care system and into independent living was successful. Many of the young adults with whom she worked left the foster care system at 18 years old and found themselves homeless, pregnant, lacking self-esteem, incarcerated, unemployed and without guidance. As a mentor, Dr. George became frustrated by the minimum amount of resources the community offered these young adults. Dr. Kishma's dream came to pass and she opened a 24-hour transitional home for young women presently in or aged out of the foster care system in Delaware. She makes a difference in their lives and makes certain that they have a safe, successful transition to adulthood and independent living.

Her diligence and passion for young women have been recognized in various newspaper articles, including the *Dover Post*, *Delaware News Journal*, *Delaware State News*, and *Milford Beacon*. She was also featured in the *Wisdom for Everyday Life, Kingdom*

Voices Magazine, Gospel 4 U Magazine, K.I.S.H. Magazine, BOND Inc., and BlogSpot's week spotlight "Fostered out of Love". In addition, she has appeared as a special guest on the Atlanta LIVE TV Show, Delmarva WBOC- ABC, Life Talk Radio Show with Coach TMB, Live TV Show Straight Talk for Women Only, 101.7 FM Radio, FoxFire Radio Show and The Frank and Travis Radio Show on Praise 105.1. Empowered Women Ministries have recognized Dr. Kishma as Woman of the Year in the category of Entrepreneurial Success as well as Zeta Phi Beta Sorority, Inc. / Theta Zeta Zeta Chapter for her outstanding involvement in the Greater Dover Community. She was also presented with the Diversity Award (2013) from the State of Delaware/Social Services, the Authentic Servant Leadership Award (2014) and New Castle County Chapter of the DSU Alumni Association 33rd annual Scholarship Luncheon for outstanding service to the Wilmington Community and the Delaware State University (2014), Church Girlz Rock; Humanitarian Award (2015), Faith Fighter Award (2016), CHOICES "Woman of the Year"(2016), State of Delaware Office of the Governor Tribute Award (2016), Business Woman of the Year (2016), Global Smashers Award (2017), I AM Baby Doll Global Award (2018), I AM Entrepreneurship Devorah Award (2018) Business Woman of the Year Award (2018) World-Changer Award (2019), I Am Fabulous Award (2019),Phenomenal Woman of the Year (2019), Mogul of the Month (2020) Woman of Influence Spot(2020), Woman of Royalty Spotlight (2022), Distinguished Women Spotlight (2022) and Phenomenal Woman Award (2022).

Dr. Kishma's passion is to empower you through the Word of God and inspire you to begin living your DREAMS. No matter what your circumstances may be, God has a purpose for your life. Dr. Kishma strives to make a difference in your life and make certain that YOU will birth EVERY DREAM God has placed on the inside. Dr. Kishma A. George is the Director of Women Destined for Greatness Mentoring Program and Visionary/Editor-in-Chief for *K.I.S.H. Magazine*.

To Contact Kishma A. George visit www.kishmageorge.com

Novita C. George

Novita C. George was born in Port-au-Prince, Haiti but was raised in St. Thomas, United States Virgin Islands. She is the proud mother of an adult daughter and son and a loving grandmother of six wonderful precious grandchildren. She is presently retired after working for 32 years as an elementary school teacher with the Department of Education in St. Thomas, United States Virgin Islands (U.S.V.I.).

Novita obtained a Bachelor of Arts in Elementary Education and a Master of Arts in Early Childhood Education, both from the St. Thomas campus of the College of the Virgin Islands (CVI), now the University of the Virgin Islands (UVI). With these degrees she secured a teaching career in St. Thomas, U. S. V. I. and taught first grade at Thomas Jefferson Elementary at Antilles School campus, substituted fourth grade at James Madison Elementary, taught second and third grades at J. Antonio Jarvis Elementary and fourth grade at Yvonne E. Milliner-Bowsky Elementary School. Additionally, she was a Pre GED teacher for Adult and Continuing Education at the J. Antonio Jarvis Elementary School campus.

She served as secretary for her 1972 alumni class of the Charlotte Amalie High School (CAHS). In the community, her favorite organization, charity and place to offer her services was at the Salvation Army where she did many chores, but her favorite chore was greeting, serving and setting at ease the guests who came to the Annual Thanksgiving Luncheon and Christmas Luncheon.

Having had such an extensive background in education and having had firsthand experience caring for and formally and informally teaching and interacting with individuals, from birth to senior adulthood, Ms. Novita George is an asset to the Board of St. Thomas Calvary Christian Academy. Secondly, she also serves as vice president on the Board of K.I.S.H. Home, Inc. She has gone beyond her call of duty to use her wealth of experience in the organization to encourage and help the young single female residents with one or no children.

Ms. Scatliffe- George is a co-author for Dreamer on the Rise; an Amazon Best-Seller Book in three categories it is a collection of 15 authors sharing their most intimate detailed experiences. It includes a foreword by the nationally renowned motivational speaker Les Brown and is endorsed by Farrah Gray, an international bestselling author, digital influencer, and business mogul.

Additionally, Ms. Scatliffe- George is an editor for K.I.S.H. Magazine, which is rising to become an asset to the world globally.

CONTACTS

Facebook: Novita George
Twitter: Novita George
Email: Novita.George21@gmail.com

Tiffany McCullough

Tiffany McCullough is the founder of *A New Revelation World Outreach Inc.*, a nonprofit organization that assists youth and their parents by offering programs that target deep-rooted issues. These programs establish structure within the family home environment, communities, and schools. She is also the owner of Early Readers Family Fun Childcare.

Tiffany studied at FAM Institute Bible College & Seminary in Baltimore, MD. She is a licensed minister, certified counselor, and licensed childcare provider. She is currently pursuing her PhD in Christian Counseling. In addition, she effectively demonstrates hope through her plays, book writings, newsletters, and other works of art.

She has written, performed, and produced various plays, such as: *Rain Down*, *He Is Risen*, *Another Chance*, *Rock-A-By-Baby*, and many others that have captivated audiences with tears, laughter, and thoughts of reflection.

As a native of Baltimore, MD, Tiffany McCullough has served as an advocate and an activist for family empowerment. She has served in various capacities by dedicating her life to help inner city youth and their families as she strives to change the projection and stigma of divorce.

Dr. Deborah Allen

Finding one's inner voice can be a liberating, awe-inspiring, and transformational experience. Fashioned to help the masses find their "fierce" is the dynamic professional Deborah Allen.

Deborah Allen is a 22X best-selling and 11X international best-selling author, speaker, certified life-coach, cleric, and CEO and creative founder of The Fierce System, a multifaceted liaison specialty centered on helping women to both find and develop their voice. Having been trained by world-renowned NSA motivational speaker Mr. Les Brown, Deborah understands the importance of strategy, development, and credible mentorship; traits she seamlessly translates to her growing clientele.

Deborah's mantra is simple: Her one and only goal is to motivate clients, helping them to create the life they were meant to live.

Refusing mediocrity on all fronts, Deborah has trailblazed a credible path for those she serves. She has served as Senior Pastor of Lighthouse Apostolic Ministries of God Church for the last 23 years and is the Executive Director of the nonprofit organization L.A.M. Ministries, Inc.

Matching servant leadership with an incredible respect for higher learning, Deborah is a Certified Life Coach and is a National Speaker Association (NSA) Speaker and a Black Speakers Network (BSN) Speaker. Her conglomerate, The Fierce System, is comprised of many platforms, including Fierce TV, Radio, and blog as well as the Fierce Voices of Destiny Program where she mentors, develops, and creates strategic alignment between clients and their true life's calling. She is the Visionary and CEO of Igniting The Flame Publishing, Visionary Coaching & Consulting Group LLC and Deborah Allen Enterprise.

Deborah proudly attests that women are at the heartbeat of all she does and that it is her desire to see them be strong, fierce, and know that they can truly achieve their dreams and walk in purpose. When she is not out helping women to come alive, rebuild, shift and find themselves again, Deborah is a valued asset to her communal body and a loving member of her family and friendship circles.

Dr. Deborah Allen. Energizer. Organizer. Servant Leader.

Contact Information: Apostle/Ambassador Dr. Deborah Allen
www.deborahallenfierce.com
www.ignitingtheflamepublishing.com
Email: deborahallenfierce@gmail.com
Social Media
Facebook: https://www.facebook.com/deborahallenfierce
Instagram: https://www.instagram.com/deborahallenfierce/
Twitter: https://twitter.com/deborahallenfie
YouTube: https://www.youtube.com/channel/
UCTOf0igcAxlVaneH2ZOo_Zg
2nd Website: https://deborahallenspeaker.com/

Shamika Minisee

Shamika Minisee is CEO/Founder of The Couture Career & Business Consultants, the Vice President and Co-Founder of Presidential Concrete LLC and is on a mission to help women build and grow profitable careers and companies. Trained as a Contracting Professional, she has a unique 14 year background in strategic planning, communications, and leadership, acquisition management on multi-billion development projects, research, professional and writing and business development which provides her clients with unique advantages.

As an empowerment expert dedicated to helping others fully embrace their power and honor their potential, Shamika brings a dynamic and motivational message delivered with humor, passion and inspiration. She has the makings of a major business entity with the persona, wit, and credentials to back it up. As a self-made entrepreneur she has a knack for focusing on incorporating lessons learned supporting the armed forces and process improvement in construction, engineering services and the mortgage industry while seeking employment and growing businesses.

With motivation, high-energy and poise, Shamika's WHY is to inspire, uplift and push career driven individuals and to help business CEOs create better blueprints, better business, experiences and lives.

Working on a wide range of assignments from Human Resources Research, Counter-Narcotics Anti-Terrorism, Major Items/Engineering Services, Integrated Air and Missile Defense, Health & Wellness, Construction & Process Engineering to name a few, she's able to deliver her unique range of innovation solutions across industries and appeal to mass audiences.

A native of St. Louis Missouri, Shamika relocated to the Tennessee Valley on her quest for higher education and now resides there with her husband Jason and their three children Jayden, Payton and Jason Jr. She holds a bachelor's degree in Business Administration and Management Information Systems from Alabama A&M University as well as a Masters in Management & Acquisition/Contract Management from Florida Institute of Technology, Level III Certified in Contracting, Program Level I Certification, and Six Sigma Yellow Belt Certification.

Memberships include: Delta Sigma Theta Sorority Incorporated, Huntsville Free Dental Clinic Board of Officers, and Sickle Cell Leadership Consortium National Board. In her spare time she helps people with personal development services to include resume writing, business planning, and job search and placement opportunities.

Let's stay in touch: linktr.ee/shamikaminisee

Setsu McClendon

Purpose Coach

Setsu McClendon gives people a sense of purpose through empowerment. In her role as a certified life coach, she enjoys transforming her life experiences and overcoming challenges, into support systems and tools. To help others determine their life purpose and embrace abundant living through authenticity. Through her work, she inspires clients and audiences around the world to be focused, driven, and purposeful. To keep her fire ignited, she is passionate about helping others achieve success in their lives in all areas. Intercession and prophecy are powerful tools in this hour as she understands the power of prayer and the Word of GOD.

Contact Information:
IG: SetsuMotivates
Facebook: Setsu.McClendon
Facebook Page/Group: Dunamis Women Network
Email: info@setsumotivates.com

Tyneise Seaborough

Tyneise is the founder of Tyneise Global, where we are being about our Father's business.

Tyneise Seaborough is a demonstrator of the power of the Kingdom of God, a dispenser of God's glory, and one marked by the fire of God. She comes in the power of Elijah and the spirit of Ezekiel. Miracles, signs, wonders, fire, and the glory of God distinguish her from your average minister of the gospel.

Some have labeled her as a John the Baptist crying out in the wilderness, a teacher like the Apostle Paul, and a howitzer (military weapon). She delivers a message of holiness and encourages others to have a reverential fear of God.

God has raised her up as a leading prayer general in warfare prayer, tactics and strategies. She comes from a dynamic lineage of ministers. The gift of healing flows through her and miracles, signs, and wonders follow her ministry. Vision returning, the lame walking, testimonies of abnormal cells being healed, blood pressure being regulated, and those with metal rods regaining their range of motion.

Contact information:

www.tyneiseglobal.com
email: tyneiseglobal@gmail.com
IG: @tyneiseglobal
FB: @tyneiseglobal

Fedora Elie Ndovie

Fedora Elie Ndovie is a multi-diverse Haitian- American woman of God, a "Mother to Nations". Mrs. Ndovie is an Apostle and Co-Founder of Chosen Vessel of God International Ministry of Malawi Africa as well as Chosen Vessel of God nonprofit organization, an organization that focuses on the younger generation of tomorrow. She stands alongside her husband, Pastor and Prophet Elijah Ranvin, Ndovie and her two boys, Theodor and Prosper. By profession she is a nurse. Mrs. Ndovie has been a credible celebrity entrepreneur in the beauty industry. TV co-host for "Beauty Enhancing Beauty Repair". Guest speaker for "Tap on" radio and Elevation TV Network. As well as Published writer in New Being Queen Magazine. Lastly Co-host of Chosen Vessel of God TV/Radio in London UK.

Co-Founder of Chosen Vessel Of God International Ministry

Email: ChosenVesselWorship21@gmail.com.

Claudine Noel

Claudine Noel is a Haitian American native of Spring Valley, NY. She is the daughter of Mr. Jean-Claude and Nicole Noel, big sister to David and Alexander Noel and an auntie to several nieces and nephews.

In 2003, Claudine graduated from Bennett College for Women, in Greensboro, NC, with a Bachelor of Arts degree in Mass Communications. Upon graduation, she worked with Young Life Greensboro outreach ministries from May 2003 to May 2006. She began a career in manufacturing in January 2008.

Claudine was licensed as a Minister of the Gospel by Shiloh Baptist church in Plainfield, NJ. She served as one of the ministers in The New Young Peoples' Department (N.Y.P.D.) ministry. Claudine believes one should develop a solid foundation of one's relationship with Christ at a very young age in order to have a sound and strong Christian life in the future; her life shall be and is dedicated to this task. Today is she is under the mentorship of Apostle Jeffrey & Pastor Shanell Thompson of Deliverance to

Kingdom Building Ministries in Somerset, NJ.

CONTACT INFORMATION

EMAILS: chosenvesselworship2021@gmail.com or
thenoelgroupllc@gmail.com
WEBSITE: thenoelgroupllc.inteletravel.com
YOUTUBE CHANNEL: C's CORNER
INSTAGRAM: CCCs.CORNER

Prophetess Shaunte D Haslem - Jones

Hello everybody, foremost I am an ambassador of Jesus Christ. I am an Christian content creator and mentor. I am an author, song writer, and CEO of Divine Inspire LLC. I enjoy reading, interior decorating, and growing flowers. I am a mother of five children and currently reside in Warner Robins, Ga with husband Johnny Jones jr.

Contact Information: Email: divineinspire.shauntejones@gmail.com

Linktr.ee/FaithFaVor5